Chorley
Then & Now
In Colour

Jack Smith

First published in 2013

The History Press
The Mill, Brimscombe Port
Stroud, Gloucestershire, GL5 2QG
www.thehistorypress.co.uk

© Jack Smith, 2013

The right of Jack Smith to be identified as the Author
of this work has been asserted in accordance with the
Copyrights, Designs and Patents Act 1988.

All rights reserved. No part of this book may be reprinted
or reproduced or utilised in any form or by any electronic,
mechanical or other means, now known or hereafter invented,
including photocopying and recording, or in any information
storage or retrieval system, without the permission in writing
from the Publishers.
British Library Cataloguing in Publication Data.
A catalogue record for this book is available from the British Library.

ISBN 978 0 7524 9315 2

Typesetting and origination by The History Press
Printed in India.

CONTENTS

Acknowledgements   4

About the Author   4

Introduction   5

Chorley Then & Now   6

ACKNOWLEDGEMENTS

In researching for new photographic material for this second edition of *Chorley Then & Now*, I have to thank the following businesses and individuals for their assistance and co-operation in providing photographs to use and/or specialist information as relevant. I must also refer to those persons mentioned in my acknowledgements in the 2001 edition of the book. My thanks to: the *Chorley Guardian* newspaper for permission to use photographs bought by readers over the years and given/loaned to me; the local photographers of yesteryear who first recorded what the town looked like 100 years ago; to my late friends' collections of photographs passed to myself: John & Evelyn Smith; Jack Rawlinson; Tom Leach of Horwich; Alderman/Councillor Charles Williams; Jock Shaw; Les Chapman. Also the late George Birtill, OBE, friend and mentor, for copies of photographs from his private collection.

In addition, thanks to Chorley Golf Club; P. Briggs and S. Harman at Washington Hall International Fire and Rescue Training Centre; Sandra Bannister of Bizspace Ltd; Coppull Mill; and Chorley Council Officers for information. Thanks to Jim and Pat Monks, Barry and Teresa Holding, Bob and Pat Catterall in Chorley, and Wilf and Norma Culshaw, now in Portugal, for their continued support and encouragement. Finally, thanks to my partner Barbara Morgan for her patience, digital photographic work, and computer skills.

ABOUT THE AUTHOR

Jack Smith has lived in Chorley most of his life, his family roots being in the railway town of Horwich near Bolton, where he served an engineering apprenticeship at the famous Horwich Locomotive Works, learning the technical side of his trade at the Railway Mechanics Institute. From the mid-1950s to mid-1960s he served as an Engineer Officer with the P&O Company on passenger and cargo ships to the Far East and Australia. He also served for two years on the troopship *Empire Fowey*, travelling to locations from Gibraltar to Hong Kong.

Back on shore he spent many years in mill maintenance and latterly worked at Chorley's Royal Ordnance Factory as Systems Auditor. As its unofficial historian, Jack went on to advise and co-author the book *A History of ROF Chorley* with Manchester University Archaeological Department.

His interest in archaeology and history saw him as one of the three founders of the Chorley and District Historical and Archaeological Society in 1953. He was secretary for thirty-six years and is now president. Jack also lectures throughout the North West and is a panel member of the Council for British Archaeology/North West Region, Industrial Archaeology. He is also a U3A committee member and the programme organiser for BAE Warton Industrial Archaeology and Railway Society.

To date, Jack has had eleven books published, half of those being about Chorley. He is currently researching the history of a local mill and a former Ministry of Supply ammunition depot.

INTRODUCTION

Chorley developed in the sixteenth century. A plan of the town in the mid-eighteenth century shows a church with side streets running off the main street (later Market Street). There were small outlying communities also, where the present Botany, Moor Road and Bolton Street areas are today. All these communities eventually joined up as the town grew through the nineteenth century. The first steam-powered cotton mills and the Lancaster Canal to the east of the town were built in the later 1790s. The railway was connected to Chorley from Bolton in 1841, then on towards Preston in 1843.

The removal of nineteenth-century property has been one of the big changes in Chorley, with former weavers' cottages being built over. Many terraced streets have gone, such as those off Bolton Street and Moor Road. The first Town Hall in Chorley, dating from 1802, was replaced by our present Town Hall in 1879, but the old building was only demolished in the 1930s. Our Victorian police station was replaced in the mid-1960s.

Chorley was once a major cotton spinning town, with at one time over twenty mills. In 2010, the last working mill was demolished and I was given the last working shuttle from a Lancashire loom which worked for a special order there. There are three three-storey mills remaining locally; one is preserved and listed, Cowling Mill teeters on the brink of survival, and Widdows Canal Mill is now a shopping complex. Fortunately one mill chimney has survived, largely due to my intervention or 'pestering' of certain local councillors! Another of the town's spinning mills has become a busy shopping centre called Botany Bay, which attracts many visitors to the town.

Until the 1990s Chorley had the Royal Ordnance Factory. Established in 1939 and opened by King George VI, it produced ammunition until winding down in 2002. Since then, the biggest housing development in Lancashire has been taking place on the site: the building of a complete new village called Buckshaw. With this development, a new railway station was opened in October 2011. Commercial workplaces are also a feature of this new village. Also on this site, two sixteenth-century halls – Buckshaw Hall and Worden Hall – have both been restored.

The town centre itself has seen some pedestrianisation, improvements to the market stalls and a shopping mall, even a new town centre bypass road (built during the 1990s). There is a new bus station 'interchange' closer to the railway station which itself was revamped some years ago.

Today we have a town which, despite some loss of historical character and heritage, still has Astley Hall and Park, the new Yarrow Valley Country Park and Healey Nab. We have our two markets, the covered market and the 'Flat Iron' (or cattle market), and streets with less traffic. We have new Civic Offices and a good library in the former Grammar School in Union Street. We also have a new landmark in the form of a marble spire on the Preston Temple of the Church of Latter Day Saints.

Chorley has changed considerably from 'Then' to 'Now', and continues to do so. By recording some of the changes here, I hope to rekindle nostalgic memories of what things were like not too long ago for some, and stimulate historical enquiry in others.

Jack Smith, June 2012

CHORLEY TOWN CENTRE

THE EARLIEST ILLUSTRATION of Chorley is from a painting from around 1820. This photograph from about 100 years later, taken at a similar location to the painting, shows, to the right, the old Town Hall adorned with flags for the town's 'Walk of Witness'. Beyond the old Town Hall is Union Street and Church Brow/Water Street, the route of the stagecoach through the town. To the left, today's Town Hall opened in 1879. Park Road is left of centre in the distance, the opening of which re-routed stagecoaches away from the steep up and down climb through 'Chorley Bottoms' (Water Street).

THE 2012 VIEW looks in a similar direction. The flower planters in the middle of the carriageway are where the right side footpath and spectators are in the old picture. The old buildings hid the parish church of St Laurence until demolition and road widening in the later 1930s.

THE PARISH CHURCH OF ST LAURENCE

THE PARISH CHURCH OF ST LAURENCE

THE OLDEST BUILDING in Chorley, the parish church of St Laurence, has its recorded origins in the fourteenth century, although an earlier church may have stood on the site. The old families of the town such as the Chorleys, Gillibrands, Standishes and the Charnocks all worshipped here and are buried within the church. Myles Standish, who sailed to the new colonies with the Pilgrim Fathers, is also associated with the church, which only became independent from the mother church in Croston in 1793. During 1868 the church, with its nave and tower, was enlarged by the building of the two aisles.

IN 1964 CHURCH Brow was closed to traffic and became a stepped footpath and the church gates were reset at an angle. In the 1980s and '90s the churchyard was cleared of burials and new parish rooms were built during the late 1990s adjoining the east end of the church, seen to the right in today's photograph. A foundation stone from the former Parish Institute, laid in 1905, was saved by the author during demolition in the 1970s. In the author's keeping for two decades, it was presented back to the church, and was built into the new church rooms in the 1990s, as a historical reminder of the existence of the former Parish Church Institute on Park Road.

THE TOWN HALL

CHORLEY'S ORIGINAL TOWN Hall, built in 1802, had a 'butter market' for local farm produce at ground-floor level, along with the police station of the time. Upstairs were the offices of the town's Board of Governors. It was converted into shops following the building of the new Town Hall in 1879 and subsequently demolished in the 1930s. The 'butter market' survived for some years, having been transferred to the cellars of the new building, with access from Mealhouse Lane.

TODAY, THE TOWN Hall frontage has hardly changed, although chimneys and railings have gone, as have the decorative lamp posts. Tarmac has replaced cobbles and in 2010 a disabled access ramp to the main door was built and a lift installed. Today, much of local government business is done in the new Civic Offices in Union Street.

THE TOWN HALL

DEMOLITION OF THE OLD ROYAL OAK INN

DEMOLITION OF THE OLD ROYAL OAK INN

IN THIS 1937 view we look out from St Thomas Road across Market Street to the old Royal Oak being demolished, it being part of the old Town Hall block of buildings which were removed so that the main road (Market Street) could be widened. In the background, the Odeon Cinema, opened in 1938, is being built. Note the Odeon 'tower' behind the demolition work, plus windows in the new building.

THE CARRIAGEWAY OF Market Street is now three lanes wide and the 'new' Royal Oak, to the right, has been largely converted into shops and office premises. The hotel was once the centre of civic functions in Chorley, as well as being a prestigious hotel and also a popular venue in the 1940s with the USAAF forces at Washington Hall. The Royal Oak was so popular with the Americans, in fact, that one of the hotel bars was named the 'American Bar' after them – a name which was retained for some fifty years or so after the end of the war, when the USAAF forces left Chorley. Today the former Royal Oak is no longer the town's foremost hotel, and is much reduced in size.

TOWN GREEN TO TOWN HALL SQUARE

BEHIND THE TOWN Hall is St Thomas's Square, known locally as Town Hall Square, around which were auctioneers' offices and the Victorian police station which incorporated the courtroom. In the 1920s the Ribble Bus Company used the Square with their Leyland-built vehicles, before a town bus station was built. On a personal note, my parents lived behind the police station buildings and I grew up with a view of the old police station and yard, as well as Town Hall Square, from my bedroom window.

TOWN HALL SQUARE today is much reduced, with the modern 1960s six-storey police station to the left, the court building in the centre and on the right a corner of the Town Hall, the 'mayor's parlour' entrance. The 'Town Hall Square' was originally 'Town Green' during the seventeen century, where, by the Market Cross, regular markets were held. There is historical evidence that at least one wife was sold at the Cross! The town's cenotaph, in Astley Park, was modelled on the old Market Cross style.

FORMER TURNPIKE ROAD TO FOOTPATH

CHURCH BROW, 1964. With the parish church gates to the left of centre and the Town Hall tower just visible through the trees to the right, we are looking back up the Brow. The old road is being blocked, using shale and ashes from local mills to build up the embankment which would support the widened Park Road, the main A6 trunk road. In the 1960s the building to the left became The Swan with Two Necks pub. Despite the road widening, however, traffic through Market Street remained excessive and was eased only with the building of the town bypass in the 1990s and with some pedestrianisation of Market Street and other town centre streets.

THE NEW EMBANKMENT could perhaps benefit from some terraced planting and seating close to the top of the steps by the parish church. It has also been mooted that the embankment should be removed and opened to traffic again!

WATER WORKS – FOUNDRY – CORN MILL

ST THOMAS'S ROAD was once a narrow lane running west towards Euxton via Ackhurst. On the south side in Dole Lane was Chorley's first (very limited) waterworks, set up in the 1840s, using a steam-driven water pump to raise water from a well to an elevated water tank, from which water fell by gravity to a piped system to houses and shops nearby. This closed when Chorley's waterworks on Healey Nab opened. The original waterworks was, sequentially, a foundry, barracks, cotton mill and lastly a corn mill. The old photograph shows the tower of the Sumner's Corn Mill in the 1960s and the old cottage at the end of Devonshire Road which was used as a 'steward's' house. The tenants of the Gillibrand estates paid their rents here.

THE CORN MILL, demolished in the 1980s, was replaced by a new multi-office block. I undertook an archaeological dig and survey on the site to find more evidence of the mill and cottage's history. The findings consolidated largely what was already known, and revealed new features relating to the old cottage. Demolition of the former mill building, which adjoined the old cottage, allowed me to investigate the site and revealed blocked windows and doorways at the cottage's gable end, as well as traces of the walls of former old buildings, long since demolished. Close by, part of a stone engine bed was found, plus traces of slag from the site's former foundry.

HIGH STREET BUILDINGS

THERE IS A sense of déjà vu about this pair of photographs, separated by seventy-five years. The older 1937 view shows buildings fronting onto Market Street as well as the rear of the old Royal Oak, minus its roof slates, being demolished (see page 12 also). To the right is the new Odeon Cinema, set back from Market Street. The new Royal Oak has yet to be built but the rubble pile would eventually become its car park.

THE NEW ROYAL Oak became Chorley's premier hotel when completed in 1939. Its rear car park gave way to shops fronting onto Cleveland Street and High Street. The car park was gradually built over again during the early years of the new millennium, with shops fronting on to High Street. But in May 2012 they were badly fire-damaged and had to be demolished, as my photograph (taken shortly after the fire) shows. Their clearance replicated the 1937 view of a cleared site, prior to rebuilding once again.

ELEPHANTS AND WOOLWORTH'S

THE UNUSUAL SIGHT of elephants in Chorley! They had come by rail to the goods yard by the town station watched by many children. Advertising a visiting circus, they were walked in procession down Chapel Street, via St Georges Street then Market Street and into Fazackerley

Street. Woolworth's store is clearly seen, with banks on either side: the District Bank to the right and Williams Deacon's to the left. Both buildings are still banks but the stylish architectural features were lost when they were rebuilt.

In the old Williams Deacon's Bank the walls were covered with decorative wooden panelling, which matched the counters. It was like the inside of some grand manor house. Although not known at the time of demolition, I later found out that this panelling was sold to an American customer, and exported to the USA. I have often wondered if the purchaser was ever at Washington Hall with the USAAF forces in the 1940s!

AN ARGOS STORE has replaced Woolworth's, but the Art Deco frontage survives, one of only two in the town today (after the January 2012 demolition of the Plaza Cinema building). The Bank of Scotland to the left and National Westminster on the right now flank Argos, and St Mary's Church tower is seen above the store. Market Street and Fazackerley Street are now mostly pedestrianized.

ST MARY'S CHURCH

ST MARY'S CHURCH, as viewed from the west side. It was built in addition to the 1774 Weldbank Church of St Gregory which saw extensions built by 1813. Following a population increase in Chorley, and despite a small chapel being created in Chapel Street in 1847, a new church was needed. Land for this was bought in 1851 at Mount Pleasant. The new church

ST MARY'S CHURCH

was designed by Joseph Hansom, and was opened in 1854. This had two floors: a church at ground level and a school upstairs, eventually having three floors. The tower was added in 1894. Extensive alterations designed by Messrs Pugin & Pugin took place in 1909.

TODAY'S VIEW IS from a little further away to create a wider view, which shows the relocated bowling green adjoining the church club. Limited new housing stands on the site of the former school and church club. To the right a new presbytery can be seen. The new Parish Club (off the modern view and to the left) has been built on the former site of a popular venue for dances, drama, and many other events. This was St Mary's Hall. However, the new club provides more modern facilities.

MARKET STREET, CHAPEL STREET CORNER

HORSE TRAFFIC DATES this view up Market Street from the bottom end of Chapel Street to the 1900s. On the left can be seen the railings fronting St Mary's Church presbytery garden. In the distance, note how narrow the carriageway is between the two Town Halls. As yet, neither the Woolworth's store nor the Canon Crank Commemorative Arch has been built.

ONE HUNDRED YEARS later the scene is little changed, except for the repositioning of the line of shops on the right, which were rebuilt further back in the 1960s to straighten out the 'bulge' which made Market Street narrower at that point. The presbytery and its garden are built over; the site now accommodates offices and Lloyds TSB Bank fronting onto Market Street.

HEAVY TRAFFIC IN MARKET STREET

TRAFFIC QUEUES IN Market Street during the 1950s and '60s were frequent, for it was the main A6 trunk. Heavy goods vehicles, buses, coaches and, increasingly, cars all used Market Street, day and night. Day trips from the Midlands to Southport, Blackpool or the Lake District added to the volume during holiday periods. Northbound queues often stretched back to the south for a mile in the mornings and southward-bound traffic again in the evenings. The Theatre Royal, later to become the Royal Cinema, subsequently demolished in the 1960s, is the tall building in the centre of the photograph.

HEAVY TRAFFIC IN MARKET STREET

THE ROYAL CINEMA was replaced by Chorley's first supermarket, run by Messrs Whelan, and in turn the building held Chorley's first McDonald's. The building and whole block await redevelopment. Today, traffic is minimal in Market Street due to the 1990s town bypass and partial pedestrianisation.

THE 'BIG LAMP' CORNER

THE 'BIG LAMP' CORNER

THE SOUTH END of Market Street formed a three-way junction, with its continuation into Bolton Street along the 'trunk' road to Manchester and the road to Wigan along Pall Mall. A large decorated gas lamp was erected in the 1860s at the junction and 'the Big Lamp' area became a popular meeting place to watch the comings and goings of people and traffic. This 1954 view shows a procession at the end of Pall Mall, escorting the town mayor to church. In the middle distance is the Royal Cinema, with the Town Hall in the distance.

OUR PRESENT-DAY photograph shows Bolton Street to the right, forming the junction with Market Street/Pall Mall. The shops on the left side have now all been demolished.

ST GEORGE'S PRIMARY SCHOOL

THE NATIONAL SCHOOL, better known as St George's Primary School, dated from 1825 and stood on 'the Big Lamp' corner. A school extension/institute to the right of the school buildings was built in Pall Mall. This corner block site also contained the fire and ambulance stations as well as the town abattoir. Eventually the area became rundown and ripe for

ST GEORGE'S PRIMARY SCHOOL

redevelopment, with relocation of the emergency services, closure of the abattoir and a new school for St George's pupils. There followed much speculation about the cleared 'Pall Mall Triangle' site and its redevelopment.

EVENTUALLY THE COOPERATIVE

Society erected a supermarket with offices, but occupancy of the site has changed several times, lastly being used by Q&S Fashions. This store closed in 2011 and the whole Pall Mall Triangle saga is due to begin again. The site is to be used for a new ASDA supermarket following the demolition of the existing building, which itself was only built in the 1990s! Demolition of the Pall Mall/ Bolton Street corner building began at the time of writing, in November 2012. We wait to see if indeed the Pall Mall Triangle will get its ASDA.

A REPAINT FOR 'THE BIG LAMP'

WE VISIT THE Big Lamp again and see its splendour restored as it is repainted. The children surrounding the painters might have attended the school mentioned previously. In this view we look from Pall Mall beyond the lamp to shops at the start of Bolton Street, with Halton's Tailors at No.1, and Whittle's Grocers at No.3; at No.5 is Messrs J. Ainsworth's drapery shop. Note the signposts on the lamp pointing to Preston, Wigan and Bolton. The gas lamp was sadly removed in the 1940s although it could have been converted to use electricity.

THE THREE-WAY junction at the Big Lamp was made into a crossroads and a new access road from George Street was created, following demolition of the shops. Our present view is taken from approximately the same place, showing a new but much less ornate Big Lamp standing on the new roundabout.

CHANGES IN LYONS LANE

WHEN CHORLEY'S TOWN centre bypass was built in the late 1990s, part of its south-westerly end incorporated the former Lyons Lane, shown here in 1958. On the left is the Victoria pub on the corner of Brooke Street, then Brooke Street itself. At the top left-hand corner is the town's one remaining factory chimney, saved despite the mill having been demolished. The author was involved with saving the chimney, it being a reminder of Chorley's cotton industry heritage. Now part of Morrisons supermarket complex, it carries the highest advertisement in Chorley. On the right is a large stone-built cotton mill, one of Chorley's earliest steam-powered mills; also visible here is Standish Street/Lyons Lane junction.

CHANGES IN LYONS LANE

OUR MODERN SCENE is totally different; the houses and mills have gone and the old Lyons Lane has become the right-hand carriageway of the bypass. Also to the right of today's view, the end of Standish Street is just visible. Where Timothy Lightoller's cotton mill once stood a new car showroom is located, whilst in the centre is Morrisons supermarket, with the former Victoria Mill Chimney now preserved. The roundabout, also in the centre, is at the bottom of Brooke Street.

LYONS LANE LOOKING NORTH

THIS VIEW ALONG Lyons Lane, from 1962, is looking in the opposite direction to the previous picture. The houses in the centre are the same ones, at the end of Brooke Street, in the distance. The building to the right is another pub, the Green Man Still. Just beyond the

LYONS LANE LOOKING NORTH

pub was a car park which was used by management of the adjoining Victoria Mill when it was worked by Messrs Gainsborough-Cornard Knitwear. Prior to demolition the mill was used by Pennine Cleaners Ltd.

THE GREEN MAN is the only original building remaining at this location, although it has now become a business premises. All the terraced houses are gone and the town centre bypass has replaced them. Just past the white building, part of the Morrisons supermarket can be seen and beyond that is Brooke Street, where a new roundabout has been created.

STANDISH STREET/ LYONS LANE JUNCTION

STANDISH STREET RECALLED! Many of the cottages on both sides dated from the mid-nineteenth century and were built by the owners of the street's two mills, which were run by the sons of Timothy Lightoller, grandfather of *Titanic*'s second officer and survivor Charles

STANDISH STREET/LYONS LANE JUNCTION

Herbert Lightoller (see the Bolton Road to Yarrow Bridge section which follows). There was also a pub called the Hare and Hounds, nicknamed the 'War Office' due to the numerous fights that took place. This 1954 photograph shows the Lyons Lane junction, where the 'Halt' sign stands.

TODAY THE HOUSES and pub are gone and the street is no longer joined to Lyons Lane. Brooke Street is to the right, beyond the roundabout. On the north side was the remaining mill chimney, again run for some time by the Lightoller family of Yarrow House. Although Lightoller's number one mill has been lost, along with Victoria Mill, the number two still stands in Standish Street. Sadly, however, its aesthetic appearance is spoiled by telephone aerials today, as are many old buildings. The south side of the street now has car showrooms, a parking area and a maintenance garage.

HANDLOOM WEAVERS' COTTAGES

CHORLEY'S COTTON INDUSTRY had its beginnings in the mid-1700s when domestic spinning and weaving was carried out. Some parts of the town by the mid/late 1800s saw the building of many cellar dwellings, which were used for the domestic trade until the building of powered mills. The Bolton Street/Bolton Road area of town had these type of cottages, particularly

HANDLOOM WEAVERS' COTTAGES

in King Street and Queen Street. This view was taken in the mid-1950s and looks down Queen Street towards what was Victoria Mill. The mill chimney (now saved) is visible to the left over the old property.

TODAY'S VIEW LOOKS toward that same mill chimney, the mill now demolished along with the cottages. In their place the mill site is occupied by a Morrisons supermarket, and the old cottages have been replaced by council property.

WATER STREET GASWORKS

THE GASWORKS IN the town was set up in Water Street (Chorley Bottoms), in the early nineteenth century, following a successful street lighting trial in 1818 in Standish Street. The company, owned by the Lightoller family, mill owners in that street, produced excess gas

WATER STREET GASWORKS

for mill lighting, and utilised this to light several street lamps by gas for the first time. This illumination of a town street led to the setting up of a gasworks to supply the town with gas. Our old view from 1956 shows the main retort house furnace plant with its coal-loading gantry. A by-product of the process was coke, which was tipped down the steep hillside to the left of the picture, like a scree (and as boys we made 'sledges' to slide down the 'coke rucks').

FOLLOWING CLOSURE AND subsequent demolition/decontamination work, the site of the works has been developed for housing. Trees now abound over the former coke stacks.

CHORLEY 'BOTTOMS' AND HOLLINSHEAD STREET

HOLLINSHEAD STREET COTTAGES stood to the north side of the street, which adjoined Water Street. I often passed this way on my way to primary school at the Hollinshead Street School. Many of my school friends lived in these houses. In the distance, in Stump Lane, was Chorley's tallest chimney, at the town 'Destructor' which burned all types of rubbish collected from around

CHORLEY 'BOTTOMS' AND HOLLINSHEAD STREET

the town by the refuse men. It was demolished brick by brick in about 1951, which I witnessed daily for a time. At the top of the hill to the left are three houses set back with garden wall frontage.

IN 2012 WE look at the same view, with the camera slightly more to the right. To the left, all the old cottages are gone but the three garden houses remain. To the right is Chorcliffe House, home of the Sylvester family, restored a few years ago. Behind Chorcliffe House was a large garden where a sort of open-air amphitheatre was created, and where plays took place – all within the garden of the eighteenth-century house. The garden area was built over a decade or so ago, and today a tall block of flats stands where the garden ampitheatre used to be.

CHORLEY FAIR

CHORLEY FAIR HAS been recorded since the seventeenth century from grants by the Lord of the Manor of Chorley. Those early fairs sold mainly animals, along with domestic and dairy goods etc. In the nineteenth century, travelling fairs came to town, with performing animals. The twentieth century saw a great change, with fairs using steam traction engines, pulling trailers and caravans, to set up side shows and roundabouts. By this time local twice-yearly fairs were established on the town 'cattle market', (nicknamed Flat Iron). Here we see two steam-driven 'galloper' rides from around 1900.

THE PAST CENTURY has seen the market site reduced in size, which in turn has led to fewer visits for the travelling fairs, and more remote locations. Here we see the fair set up in Market Street, April 2012, outside the former Woolworth's store.

CLIFFORD STREET AND CHAPEL STREET CORNER

CLIFFORD STREET CORNER with Chapel Street. Dating from the 1960s and looking north into Clifford Street from Chapel Street, to the right is the Victoria Building dating from 1903 and built as the main offices of the 'Loyal Order of Ancient Shepherds' Chorley Branch. Because of this connection the building was known as the 'Shepherds' Hall'. To the left corner, the stone building was associated with market traders for a time. In Clifford Street and to the left of the picture

CLIFFORD STREET AND CHAPEL STREET CORNER

is the tower of the former Haydock's Sawmills, located at the corner of Hill Street, just past the tower. The works latterly became Morrisons supermarket in the early 1990s.

ALTHOUGH THE TWO corner buildings are unchanged, the tower and sawmill were demolished in the later 1990s. Today, the goods access yard to the town shopping mall stands where the tower once stood, its gateway and wall visible.

THE CATTLE MARKET (OR FLAT IRON)

THE CATTLE MARKET (OR FLAT IRON)

THE CATTLE MARKET is also known as the 'Flat Iron'. Some say this nickname comes from the way cloths were held down to prevent them being blown away from market stalls – or it was due to the rolling of the surface to create a flat area? Originally a small river valley was here in the early 1800s, which was filled in after piping the stream. Our old view looks to the north side in the 1950s, when, in Union Street, Hughlock Hindle's garage was standing.

DURING THE 1990S the garage and the printworks behind it were cleared away and a new building erected which would become Chorley Borough Council Civic Offices. It still is. Also just visible is Chorley's new statuary, on the white plinth left of centre, to commemorate the Chorley Pals' losses in the First World War.

CORONATION RECREATION GROUND

CORONATION RECREATION GROUND, as it became, was an official open space in the early 1900s, and has a unique historical association. Following the Coronation of King George V and Queen Mary in 1911, they were due to tour Lancashire in 1912. This was delayed due to the King being unwell, but took place in 1913. They visited Chorley on 10 July. Arriving from Blackburn by train, they were driven to the recreation pleasure ground in Devonshire Road,

CORONATION RECREATION GROUND

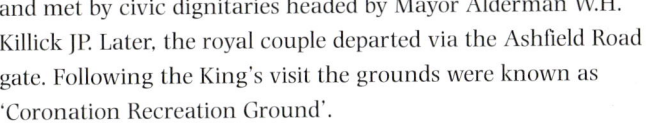

and met by civic dignitaries headed by Mayor Alderman W.H. Killick JP. Later, the royal couple departed via the Ashfield Road gate. Following the King's visit the grounds were known as 'Coronation Recreation Ground'.

TODAY'S IMAGE OF cherry blossom trees in flower compares with the winter view of this splendid avenue in the centre of the 'rec'. The avenue of trees commemorates the route taken by King George V and Queen Mary in 1913. The inset is of their majesties, but not during their Chorley visit.

ENTRANCE GATES TO ASTLEY PARK

ASTLEY PARK GATES on Park Road. The park and Hall were given to the town as a war memorial in 1919 by Reginald Arthur Tatton, the town cenotaph being built a short distance inside the gates. The old view shows the entrance to Astley Park, built after 1822, with the opening of Park Road, as it was up to 1920, when the old gateway, with its gatehouse to the right, was demolished and a new gateway built. The arched gateway was formerly the entrance to Gillibrand Hall and estate, standing on Letchworth Drive, and was removed and re-erected here, with smaller side gate pillars added, to match the main arch stonework. The words 'PRO PATRIA' are carved above the arch, with the dates 1914–1918.

THE ASTLEY GATEWAY, shown above, replaced the original entrance to Astley Park from Water Street, close to the bottom of Church Brow. The gatekeeper's cottage is to the right of the gateway, its roof being visible. The present-day gateway, as discussed opposite, is quite imposing, and totally fitting, for the whole of Astley Park was given to the town as a war memorial and accommodates the town cenotaph which, until 2012, enjoyed a simplistic open appearance. Large plaques naming the town's war dead have been added, which many people say has removed the simplicity that the site once had. As yet, the main gateway has thankfully not been altered ... so far!

ASTLEY HALL

ASTLEY HALL BEGAN life in the sixteenth century as the home of the Charnock family. It was originally built in the traditional timber frame style, around an open courtyard. It saw many additions and alterations over the centuries, yet much of the old timber framework can still be seen to the north back, courtyard, and west side. The old view looks at the south front. Oliver Cromwell allegedly slept here during his northern campaigns.

LITTLE HAS CHANGED to the front of the hall today. It has had its stonework cleaned and its many attractions have been enhanced with the conversion of the adjoining coach house into an art gallery and café. During the 1970s the author was founder chairman of the Astley Hall Society, which continues to raise money to purchase items for improvements to the hall's interior. The house is open to the public and is owned by Chorley Council.

ACKHURST BROW AND ASTLEY PARK

ACKHURST BROW TO the west of Chorley leads to Euxton village, then on to Eccleston, Croston, Ormskirk and Southport. The later 1950s view of this hill at Ackhurst Farm shows little development at this time. The farm at Ackhurst was worked by a relative of school friends, and was a place we often visited on our bikes, to 'help out' with jobs there. Besides, there was an old bus and a tower, used in wartime as a fire watcher's look-out, which were great places for young lads to have to themselves in the post-war years.

DEVELOPMENT HAS CHANGED this former country lane to a busy main road. The farm was converted to a pub/restaurant in the 1970s

and the fields were developed with office blocks and a Tesco supermarket. To the right is the west-end gateway into Astley Park, in mock timber-frame style, and once the park's head gardener's residence.

A NEW MOTORWAY VIA CHORLEY

A NEW MOTORWAY VIA CHORLEY

THE M61 CAME through Chorley's east valley at Crosse Hall in 1967. This view looks from Crosse Hall Lane bridge over the motorway construction work, northward to Froom Street bridge and Heapey Road in the distance. Talbot Mill, with its four-storey spinning rooms and 1,700 looms, was still in production then. To the right is Lower Healey, a former bleach works and army detention centre. I worked here for some years as production foreman on linoleum storage, with cutting and manufacture of pitch fibre pipes. Production later changed to tufted carpet manufacture.

THE M61 HAS been open since 1969, and the scars made in construction have now healed. Sadly we lost Crosse Hall Mill Farm, where I also helped Mr Birchall as a boy (when not required at White House Farm). The farm has been obliterated and new houses built over the site these past two years, to the left of our 2012 picture.

COWLING ROAD MILL COTTAGES

COWLING ROAD MILL COTTAGES

SOUTH-EAST TOWARDS the high moorland or the picturesque Rivington village and reservoirs, this area is well visited at all times of the year due to the variety of interests it caters for, be it a leisurely stroll, a strenuous climb or just a picnic. All are within twenty minutes of Chorley along Cowling Road, seen here in the 1960s, when the old stone mill on the bank of the canal and its cottages opposite were still in use and/or occupied. The mill was originally a spinning mill called 'Hall o'th Wood' Mill, demolished in the late 1970s along with the cottages and shop.

TODAY'S VIEW IS without character: all the old property has gone, as has its historical aspects. To the left, the site of the old mill has been built over with yet more housing, and to the right, modern sheds serve as warehouses and other manufacturing units. But the canal and its bridge and wharf are still there to enjoy.

MILL CHIMNEYS AND CANAL

HERE WE LOOK north along the canal towards Cowling Road where the mill, mentioned previously, is still standing, right of centre. The photograph dates from about 1919/20 when Chorley's cotton industry was thriving. Three mill chimneys are visible, but four mills share the three! To the left is Cowling Mill, to the right Hall o'th Wood (or Cowling Bridge Mill). The centre chimney is shared by Redan Mill and Crosse Hall Mill. Also to the right is Hall o'th Wood Farm.

MILL CHIMNEYS AND CANAL

IN TODAY'S VIEW the new houses on the site of the right-hand mill are visible. In the centre Redan Mill and Crosse Hall Mill have been demolished. Cowling Mill (now invisible due to tree growth), with its terracotta brickwork and elaborate mouldings, is not in good condition. Sadly this unlisted decorative mill of 1906, the last multi-storey mill left in the town, seems to be heading for demolition.

I worked at Cowling Mill for many years, and I have very special memories of the work done there. I know that the mill building has some interesting architectural features. Conversion of this building into living space for flats and apartments would follow what is being done elsewhere in other Lancashire mill towns. A mill conversion project such as this would be a first for Chorley, but would follow a similar project in Bamber Bridge. Sadly, however, demolition often seems the easier and less expensive way forward, as seen recently with Talbot Mill.

CANAL BRIDGE WIDENING AT BOTANY

CROSSING THE CANAL in the direction of Wheelton and Blackburn at Botany, we look at work going on at the canal bridge. It is the mid-1930s, and the original narrow road bridge was being widened to facilitate the increase in traffic over the bridge. Looking north-east, we see work in progress. In this immediate area were several public houses. Three are in this view, built (so the stories go) to 'accommodate' the canal-boat men and the warehousemen here, many of them living close by in a notorious street called 'Long Row'. The row's reputation derived

CANAL BRIDGE WIDENING AT BOTANY

from the fact that those men employed at the canal-side warehouse and on the boats both worked hard and played hard; they celebrated all-too-often in the three pubs in the community, which led to many fights between individuals and between families living close by in 'Long Row'.

THIS MODERN VIEW looks in the same direction as the old view. The bridge parapets are visible to left and right. The widening in the 1930s is recorded on these walls. Today the bridge no longer carries the main road over the canal. The bridge now serves as an alternative access to the former Canal Mill, now referred to as Botany Bay Village, a five-floor retail outlet.

BOTANY BAY IN CHORLEY

CHORLEY HAD A 'port' nicknamed 'Botany Bay', when commercial boats plied their trade along the canal system. It is said the name originated from working comparisons with the Australian penal colony! The canal was originally the 'Lancaster' from the 1790s until 1816, when the Chorley section was leased by the Leeds to Liverpool Canal. An 1820s warehouse was built at a wharf close to the road bridge, featured in the previous photograph. Here boats loaded and unloaded goods. It was a busy place during the earlier commercial canal traffic years.

BOTANY BAY IN CHORLEY

WITH THE COMING of the M61 motorway through Chorley's east valley and Botany, the old canal road bridge became redundant but was retained. A new bridge was built in 1968 which now spanned two three-lane motorway carriageways plus the canal. The warehouse was demolished. The new bridge pillars to the right are on the site of the warehouse and wharf.

EIGHT-ARCH VIADUCT

BOTANY RAILWAY VIADUCT was built in 1868 on the Wigan to Blackburn via Chorley line by the Lancashire and Yorkshire Railway. It comprised an eight-arch span with embankments each end, spanning the valley and canal. Beyond the viaduct was a cotton mill run by Messrs Widdows and Company. This survived the near total demolition of Chorley's textile mill buildings. After some years as a vehicle spares depot, the mill was eventually purchased to create a leisure/shopping complex on all five floors of the former mill, now called 'Botany Bay' and advertised on television.

EIGHT-ARCH VIADUCT

THE FORMER MILL, with new pinnacles adorning the corners, is seen by hundreds of vehicles which pass the mill to the west (left) side. A boatyard to the right of the canal runs pleasure outings on wide boats. The former embankment to the viaduct to the right is now almost invisible due to tree growth.

CHORLEY WORKHOUSE

ON EAVES LANE in Chorley a workhouse was built during the later nineteenth century, to become Chorley Union Workhouse. This led to the closure of workhouses in two local villages,

CHORLEY WORKHOUSE

Croston and Brindle. It gradually became a part of Eaves Lane Hospital, or Moorfields as it used to be called, during the 1950s when 'lodging houses' were closing down and the welfare of the elderly became of greater concern under the National Health programme. Despite these changes, the hospital itself retained a sort of stigma, with its 'workhouse' origins. The fine Victorian stone building was a sad loss when it was demolished a decade or so ago. It was suggested the building should have been preserved and converted into flats and apartments.

TODAY ALL THAT remains is the boundary wall with some old railings on top. Of the former workhouse and hospital buildings, perhaps the best examples of Victorian buildings in the town, there is no trace. The site has been completely built over with new houses.

THE CHURCH OF ST GREGORY, WELDBANK

ST GREGORY'S CHURCH of 1774 was the first Roman Catholic church to be built in the town following the period of persecution. Before this, those of the Catholic faith had to worship secretly. This was done locally in a private chapel at Higher Burgh Hall where the Chadwick

family lived, and followed the faith. The church has undergone extensions and alterations to the original. The church is built at the top of a hill, and is the highest church in the town at the junction of Burgh Lane, Weldbank Lane, and Pilling Lane. There is a primary school a short distance from the church. Burials still take place within the confines of the churchyard, and there is a gate lodge to pass when entering the grounds of the church.

TODAY'S STUDY OF the church of St Gregory's at Weldbank illustrates how the church exterior has changed little externally over the past century.

OLD COTTAGES IN BOLTON ROAD

THESE OLD COTTAGES started life in the early nineteenth century as cellar dwellings where hand weaving or spinning was done during the 'domestic' manufacturing period. Their occupants witnessed the transition from hand to machine manufacture of cotton goods. The sepia view was taken in the mid-1950s, when some cottages had been converted to shops, but some of the unaltered 'up steps' cottages are still visible. The cottages were built on what would become the main A6 trunk road running south out of the town.

DURING THE 1990s a new town centre bypass saw the demolition of this row of cottages, along with old property in the streets behind. Road widening and rebuilding with council property, set back from the road, does not allow an exact 'same spot' view today, although the street to the right in the modern view is the same as the one in the 1960s.

BOLTON ROAD AT YARROW BRIDGE

MOVING FURTHER SOUTH out of the town, we look towards Yarrow Bridge. The original Yarrow Bridge Inn formed the centre of a community. Thomas De Quincey stayed here whilst writing *Confessions of an English Opium Eater* (1821). The old inn and turnpike road

BOLTON ROAD AT YARROW BRIDGE

are now part of history. In 1822 this new section of road was built and the old road (half a mile to the right) was closed. This 1930s view with almost no traffic is in contrast with today. To the left is an entrance gateway to a large building called Yarrow House, the home of the Lightoller family, where Charles Herbert Lightoller, senior surviving officer of the *Titanic* disaster 101 years ago this year, was born.

THE SAME WALL exists today, but Albany High School stands on the site of Yarrow House. A plaque affixed to the gateway commemorates the bravery of Charles Lightoller. After the *Titanic* sank, Charles searched for survivors and gathered many lifeboats together to await rescue. He went on to command Royal Navy ships during the 1940s, and even crossed to Dunkirk in his own small boat to help evacuate the beaches.

A LANDMARK FOR TRAVELLERS!

THE NORTHERN APPROACH into Chorley along the A6 road had, from the early twentieth century, a landmark known to travellers, especially before the advent of motorways. Coming into Chorley from the north, people would be told to 'look out for the tall water tower on the

A LANDMARK FOR TRAVELLERS!

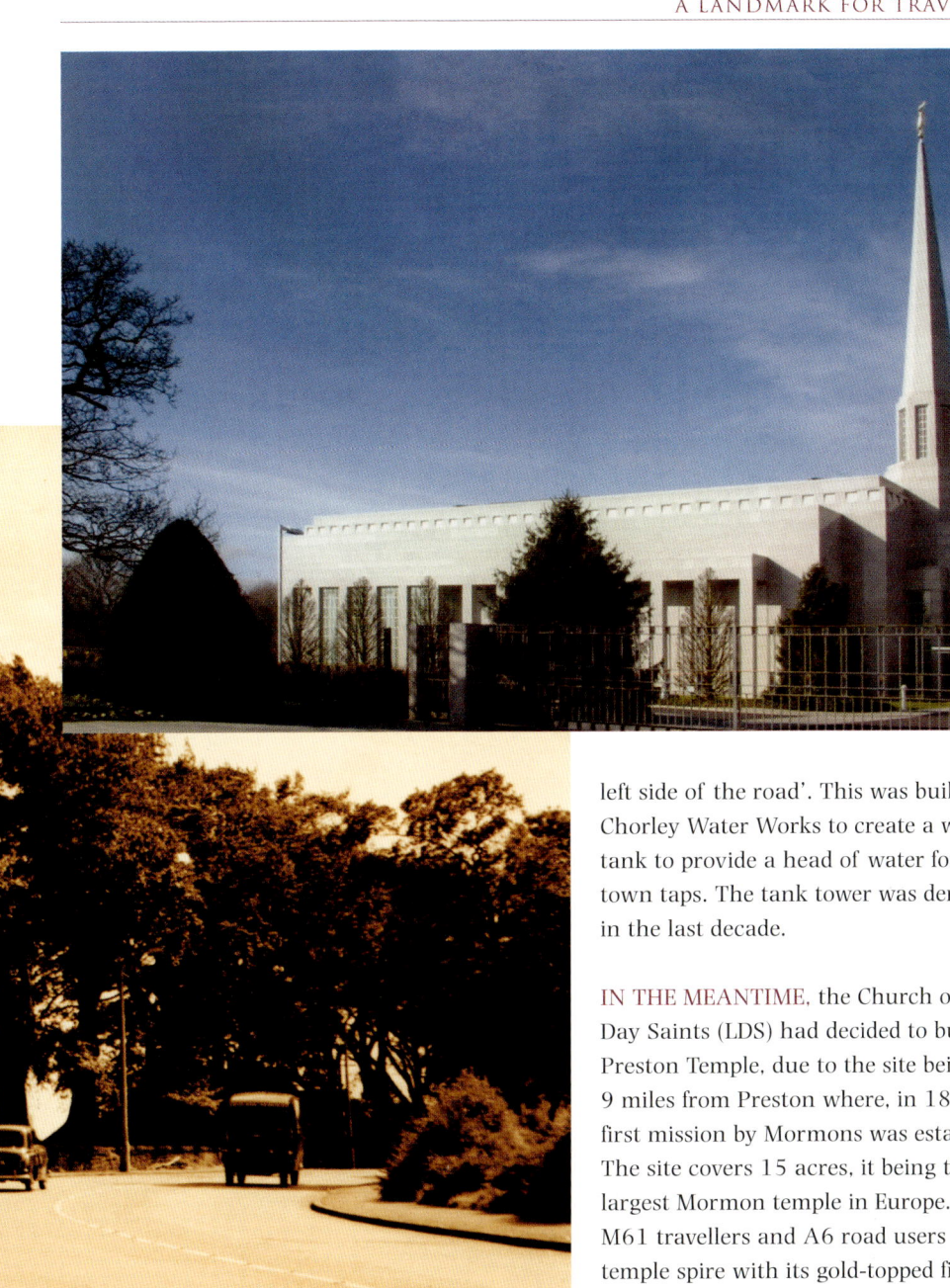

left side of the road'. This was built by the Chorley Water Works to create a water tank to provide a head of water for the town taps. The tank tower was demolished in the last decade.

IN THE MEANTIME, the Church of Latter Day Saints (LDS) had decided to build a Preston Temple, due to the site being only 9 miles from Preston where, in 1837, the first mission by Mormons was established. The site covers 15 acres, it being the largest Mormon temple in Europe. Today M61 travellers and A6 road users see the temple spire with its gold-topped figure as a landmark well worth seeing.

GREAT HOUSE BARN, RIVINGTON VILLAGE

ALSO KNOWN AS the Bottom Barn (as opposed to its counterpart, Hall Barn), this sepia view from the beginning of the twentieth century shows it when the farm was working, to the right. The hay barn (to the left) was longer than it is today and was shortened due to road

GREAT HOUSE BARN, RIVINGTON VILLAGE

widening. Both barns are of cruck frame construction probably dating back to Saxon times. Both are listed buildings and are well used: Hall Barn for dancing, concerts, teas and many other functions, while Great House Farm Barn has a souvenir and arts shop and serves teas and snacks. Both venues are popular throughout the year.

TODAY'S VIEW OF Bottom Barn was taken in March 2012 and shows people enjoying their day in this very popular village – and having tea, of course! The farmhouse is still a private dwelling, and its adjoining buildings are now a visitor centre and toilet block.

COPPULL RING SPINNING MILL, STEAM ENGINE HOUSE

THIS SPINNING MILL is one of three built by the same builder between 1900 and 1910, the last of the 'modern mills' to be built in Chorley, with the same make of engine by J. & E. Woods of Bolton to drive spinning machinery. They were: Cowling Mill in Chorley, and Mavis Mill and Ring Mill in Coppull, a borough village. Mavis Mill, twinned with Ring Mill (they shared the same chimney), has been demolished. Cowling Mill is in poor condition and, despite proposals to convert it into flats, may be demolished, regardless of its architectural merit.

COPPULL RING SPINNING MILL, STREAM ENGINE HOUSE

The engine drove a 25ft-diameter flywheel and ropes to the machinery on each floor. Sadly it was scrapped in the 1960s. (Note: a similar size engine is still working at the Wigan Pier complex.)

THE ENGINE HOUSE is a listed building and now contains small offices and displays, as shown. The steps have been built in the former driving rope race. The mill now accommodates many unit businesses and office suites.

WHITTLE SPRINGS, CANAL BASIN AND BREWERY

THE CANAL AT Whittle Springs was originally the Lancaster Canal. It was at this basin in 1818 that the Leeds to Liverpool Canal joined the Lancaster via Johnson's Hillock Locks. Whittle Springs was so called following the discovery of mineral spring water here in the nineteenth century, after which a spa hotel was built. The early twentieth century saw 'Whittle Springs Brewery' established. Canal boats transported beer in barrels and brought in brewing materials. The old brewery buildings are visible in the distance in the sepia photograph. The hotel became a private home before becoming a pub and concert venue. The brewery buildings were demolished and replaced by new houses.

THE CANAL WAREHOUSE and wharf were only demolished in the 1990s to be replaced by the houses shown in the 2012 photograph. In the distance the first of the locks on the Leeds to Liverpool Canal is visible.

CHARNOCK RICHARD PARISH CHURCH

CHARNOCK RICHARD PARISH CHURCH

ANOTHER CHORLEY VILLAGE is Charnock Richard, so named after the principal family here in the sixteenth century, the Charnocks of Charnock. One of the family, by name Richard, gave his name to the community but reversed to 'Charnock Richard'. The village community is divided into two, the other being 'Welsh Whittle', also stemming from local family names. The family home of the Charnocks was destroyed by fire in the sixteenth century, the family relocating to Astley Hall in Chorley. Park Hall became the hall of the manor, home of the Darlingtons. This hall is now a hotel and conference centre. The parish church is 'Christ Church' and features here, with four young ladies standing by the lychgate to the churchyard – date uncertain, but probably in about the 1900s.

THE LYCHGATE IS seen today in a wider view to encompass the church tower.

THE HALL ON THE HILL

HALL O'TH HILL DATES from the thirteenth century, and was originally a timber-framed hall within a moat, north of the present hall. In later years the family Gogard (or Duxbury?) moved to the new location due to the poor condition of the old house. Much timber and stone was moved uphill to the new site to use in rebuilding the new 'Hall on the Hill'. The hall was rebuilt in stone in 1724 by Thomas Willis, and owned by that family until the 1890s. It then became the nine-hole Chorley Golf Club for a time until around 1902, later becoming an eighteen-hole course in 1926. The hall was larger than today and faced south; it was altered over the years to create a frontage to the west, as we see in both views here.

THE BUILDING FRONTAGE of today shows part of the altered south side to the right. The west side remains unchanged except for its distinctive Virginia creeper. The low wall visible in the old and the new images was originally a Ha-Ha garden feature which extended around the west and the north side of the building. This was built to stop animals grazing beyond the confines of the Ha-Ha. Some local writers have referred to 'Hall o' the Hill' as 'the hall which climbed the hill', for much of it did just this. This was accomplished by the sheer hard work of men and horses, who demolished the old hall and moved the building materials up the hill to the new site.

WASHINGTON HALL, CHORLEY

ORIGINALLY BUILT AS the third hostel for employees at the new (1938) Royal Ordnance Factory close by, these buildings were never used for that purpose, two hostels being used only. In 1942 the United States Army Air Force came to the hostel, now a camp. An adjoining lane was named 'German Lane' after a local family, but the Americans had the name changed to Washington Lane and the camp then became 'Washington Hall'. Our old view shows a group of USAAF Military Police at the camp, with Jeep and Harley motorcycle.

WASHINGTON HALL, CHORLEY

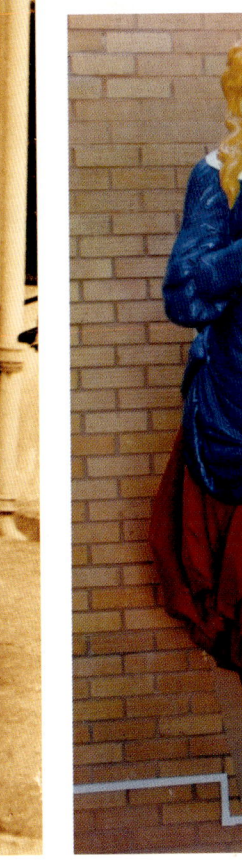

IN 2012 THE last old 1930s hostel (and camp) buildings of Washington Hall are being demolished, to enable additional changes to be made within the complex that is now Washington Hall International Fire and Rescue Training Centre. I am currently recording the demise of the old buildings and the erection of new ones. The ship's figurehead featured here was given to the USAAF in 1943, by the hostel's (camp's) architect, Sir George Grenville. In the 1970s it was replaced by a fibreglass copy, shown here in the canteen building. The restored original wooden figure is in Liverpool Maritime Museum.

If you enjoyed this book, you may also be interested in…

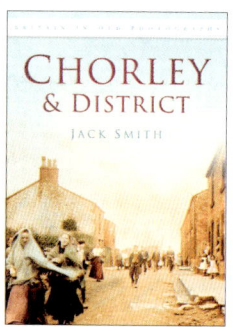

Chorley & District
JACK SMITH

Located on the eastern edge of the Lancashire plain on the banks of the River Chor, at the centre of a rich agricultural area, Chorley was a market town from medieval times. This beautifully presented book depicts the growth and prosperity which arose with the Industrial Revolution, through juxtaposing images of streets, buildings and people. The photographs feature aspects of industry such as cotton weaving and spinning; coal mining and quarrying; and canal and railway links accompanied by informative caption

978 0 7524 4948 7

Leyland Then & Now
DAVID HUNT & WILLIAM WARING

For 800 years the Leylanders had clustered around their medieval village cross, but all this changed rapidly after 1870 when the town embarked on nearly a century of phenomenal growth. *Leyland Then and Now* traces the story of these developments through a wonderful collection of old photographs, which are compared and contrasted with modern equivalents, unveiling amazing changes and unexpected similarities.

978 0 7524 7743 5

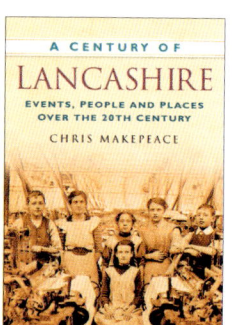

A Century of Lancashire
CHRIS MAKEPEACE

A Century of Lancashire provides a striking account of the changes that have so altered the county's appearance and records the process of transformation. Drawing on detailed local knowledge of the community, and illustrated with a wealth of black-and-white photographs, this book recalls what Lancashire has lost in terms of buildings, traditions and ways of life. It also acknowledges the regeneration that has taken place and celebrates the character and energy of local people as they move through this new century.

978 0 7509 4915 6

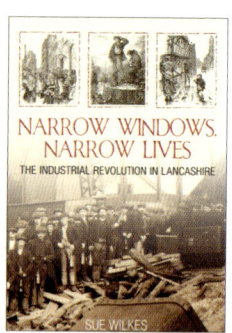

Narrow Windows, Narrow Lives: The Industrial Revolution in Lancashire
SUE WILKES

Narrow Windows, Narrow Lives recreates everyday life for the workers in factories, the bargemen, the coalminers, metal workers, navvies and glassblowers, using first-hand accounts and contemporary documents. It depicts the shocking state of the newly industrialised North and sketches the fascinating stories of those who lived through it. This book tells the real stories of life in those harsh times.

978 0 7524 4253 2

Visit our website and discover thousands of other History Press books.

www.thehistorypress.co.uk